War, Cattle, and Cowboys

Texas as a Young State

Heather E. Schwartz

Consultant

Devia Cearlock
K–12 Social Studies Specialist
Amarillo Independent School District

Publishing Credits

Dona Herweck Rice, *Editor-in-Chief*
Lee Aucoin, *Creative Director*
Marcus McArthur, PhD., *Associate Education Editor*
Neri Garcia, *Senior Designer*
Stephanie Reid, *Photo Editor*
Rachelle Cracchiolo, M.S.Ed., *Publisher*

Image Credits:

Cover, p.1, pp.2–3 Bridgeman Art Library; p.4, 5, 6 North Wind Picture Archives; p.7 LOC [LC-USF33–003139]; p.7 (sidebar) Corbis; p.8 Alamy; p.9 (top) North Wind Picture Archives; p.9 (bottom) Getty Images; p.10 The Granger Collection; p.11 (left) LOC [LC-DIG-pga–0347]; p.11 (middle) Archive.org; p.11 (sidebar) Corbis; p.12 LOC [LC-DIG-ppmsca–19520]; p.13 National Archives; p.14 North Wind Picture Archives; p.15 National Archives; p.16 The Granger Collection; p.17 Library of Congress; p.17 (sidebar) LOC [LC-DIG-ppmsca–20280]; p.18 Minnesota Historical Society; p.19 (top) LOC [LC-DIG-stereo-1s02762], p.19 (bottom) LOC [LC–USZC4–1155]; p.20 North Wind Picture Archives; p.21 Bridgeman Art Library; p.21 (sidebar) Bridgeman Art Library; p.22, 23 Bridgeman Art Library; p.24 North Wind Picture Archives; p.25 (top) Bridgeman Art Library; p.25 (bottom) DeGolyer Library ; p.26 (top) Bridgeman Art Library; p.27 Bridgeman Art Library; p.27 (sidebar) Speeches and State Papers of James Stephen Hogg (public domain); p.28 North Wind Picture Archives; p.29 (top) LOC [LC–DIG–ppmsca–13514]; p.29 (sidebar) iStockphoto; All other images Shutterstock.

Teacher Created Materials
5301 Oceanus Drive
Huntington Beach, CA 92649-1030
http://www.tcmpub.com

ISBN 978-1-4333-5050-4

Printed in China WAI002

Table of Contents

A New State

Before 1845, Texas was a free **republic**. It had gained its independence, or freedom, from Mexico nine years earlier. But in 1845, Texas was **annexed** (AN-eksd), or added to, the United States. It became the 28th state in the Union.

The next 15 years is known as the **antebellum** (an-tee-BEL-uhm) period. This was before the Civil War. During this time, Texas became more like other Southern states around it. Many settlers came to the new state from the South. These settlers brought their Southern beliefs with them. Like other Southern states, Texas grew dependent on cotton.

Texas was a slave state. Slave labor made it possible to produce cotton for a **profit**. The Texas **Constitution** of 1845 protected slavery.

slaves picking cotton

cotton wagons in Dallas, Texas

As the Texas cattle industry grew, the state became known for cattle and cowboys. Still, the traits Texas shared with the South were important. As the new state formed its own identity, these Southern traits would have a major impact on the future of the United States.

New Settlers

While Southerners made up most of the population in Texas, **ethnic** groups lived there as well. The territory always had many Mexicans because of its history and location. In the 1850s, settlers also came from Germany, Sweden, Czechoslovakia (check-uh-sluh-VAH-kee-uh), and Poland.

War with Mexico

In 1846, the Mexican-American War began. This conflict between Mexico and the United States was over the border between Texas and Mexico. Texas claimed its southern border with Mexico stretched down to the Rio Grande. Mexico said this border was located farther to the north at the Nueces (noo-EY-suhs) River.

Vaqueros brand longhorn cattle.

Early Cattle Ranching

By 1845, cattle ranching had a long history in Texas. It began in the early 1700s. The Spanish brought longhorn cattle to Texas to feed Spanish soldiers and **missionaries**. Longhorn cattle were large and strong. They often weighed 1,800 pounds (816 kg). The horns on their heads could span four feet (1.2 m).

Mexicans living in the Texas territory had special ways to handle cattle. These Mexican ranchers, called *vaqueros* (vah-KAIR-ohs), used special tools to catch cattle. One tool was called a **lariat** (LAR-ee-uht), or lasso. This was a long rope with a noose. Vaqueros would keep the lariat near their **saddle horns**. Vaqueros were brave and tough, and had a lot of **stamina**.

Early American cowboys acted and looked like Mexican vaqueros. When people from other parts of the United States moved into Texas, Mexicans taught them how to handle cattle. Vaqueros also passed on their values. Texas ranchers in the 1840s and 1850s mainly ran small businesses that supplied beef to local buyers. Ranching was a small part of the Texas economy for many years. But soon, the ranching industry would experience a **boom**.

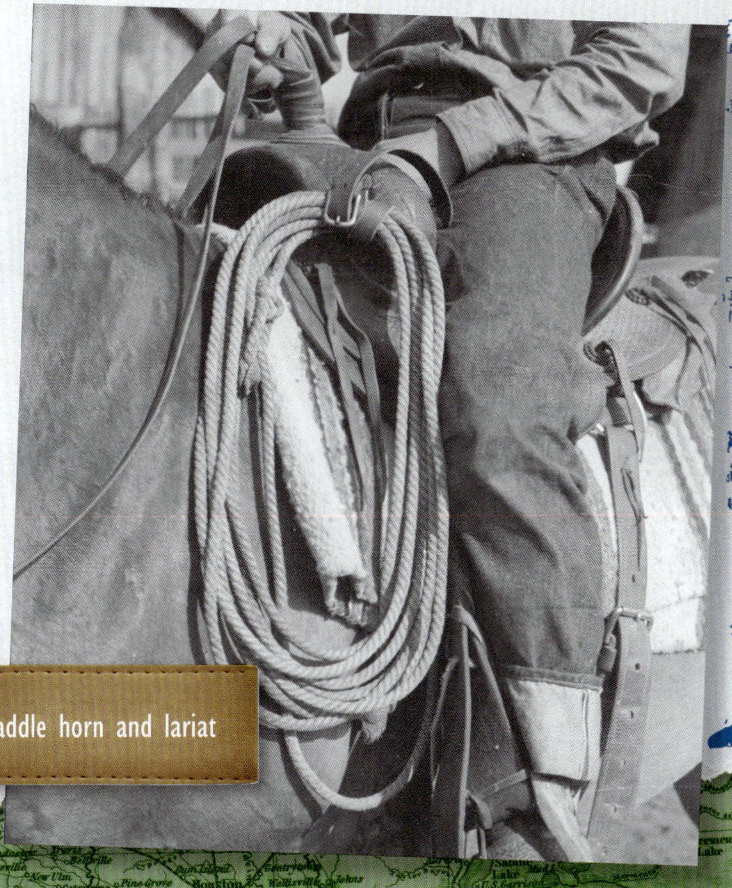

saddle horn and lariat

John Wayne became famous as a cowboy actor.

Cowboy Myths

In books and movies, cowboys are often shown living an exciting life, riding their favorite horse, and fighting American Indians daily. In reality, cowboy life was very different. They rode several different horses and rarely fought against American Indians.

Cattle Drives

Some early Texas ranchers hired cowboys to drive their cattle to other states. There, the animals would sell for more money. These cattle drives were hard and dangerous.

The Civil War

A Short Peace

America was at war with Mexico since 1846. But in 1848, the United States and Mexico signed the **Treaty** of Guadalupe Hidalgo (gwahd-l-OOP-ay hi-DAHL-goh). This ended the Mexican-American War. The treaty gave parts of Mexico to the United States.

After the treaty was signed, new debates over borders began. But this time, the conflicts were within the United States. The South wanted to expand slavery into the new western territory, but the North did not support slavery. Texas wanted to expand its border farther west. Southern states liked this idea because Texas was a slave state. Expanding the Texas border would expand slavery, too.

This map shows the expansion of slavery in Western territory after the Compromise of 1850.

A runaway slave is captured under the Fugitive Slave Act.

Both sides worried the United States would not have a balance of free and slave states. The conflict showed that the issue of slavery could tear apart the nation.

reward poster for a runaway slave

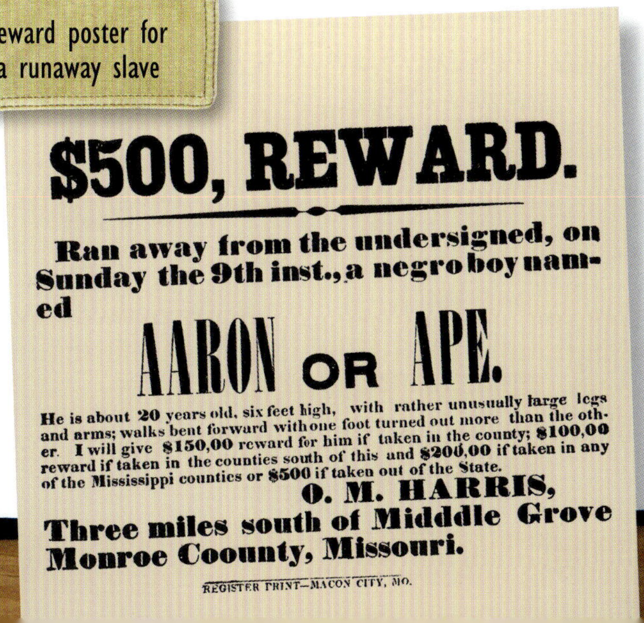

$500, REWARD.

Ran away from the undersigned, on Sunday the 9th inst., a negro boy named

AARON OR APE.

He is about 20 years old, six feet high, with rather unusually large legs and arms; walks bent forward with one foot turned out more than the other. I will give $150,00 reward for him if taken in the county; $100,00 reward if taken in the counties south of this and $200,00 if taken in any of the Mississippi counties or $500 if taken out of the State.

O. M. HARRIS,

Three miles south of Midddle Grove Monroe Coounty, Missouri.

REGISTER PRINT—MACON CITY, MO.

Compromise of 1850

The Compromise of 1850 briefly settled the conflict between the North and the South. Texas gave up some western land claims in exchange for $10 million. To keep the balance between slave and free states, California came into the Union as a free state. To satisfy the South, Congress passed the **Fugitive** (FYOO-ji-tiv) Slave Act.

Fugitive Slave Act

The Fugitive Slave Act required that fugitives and freed slaves living in Northern states be returned to their owners in the South. Antislavery people in the North hated this law. They felt it forced them to play a part in the slave system.

Tensions Rise

By 1860, slavery was still the major issue dividing the country. Many Southern states wanted to **secede** (si-SEED), or withdraw, from the Union.

In November, Abraham Lincoln was elected president of the United States. He was against slavery expanding west. This made Southerners want to secede even more. They saw their slaves as property. And they felt they should be allowed to bring their property into any American territory. In December 1860, South Carolina seceded from the Union. In January 1861, Mississippi, Florida, Alabama, Georgia, and Louisiana followed. By that summer, the rest of the South had also seceded.

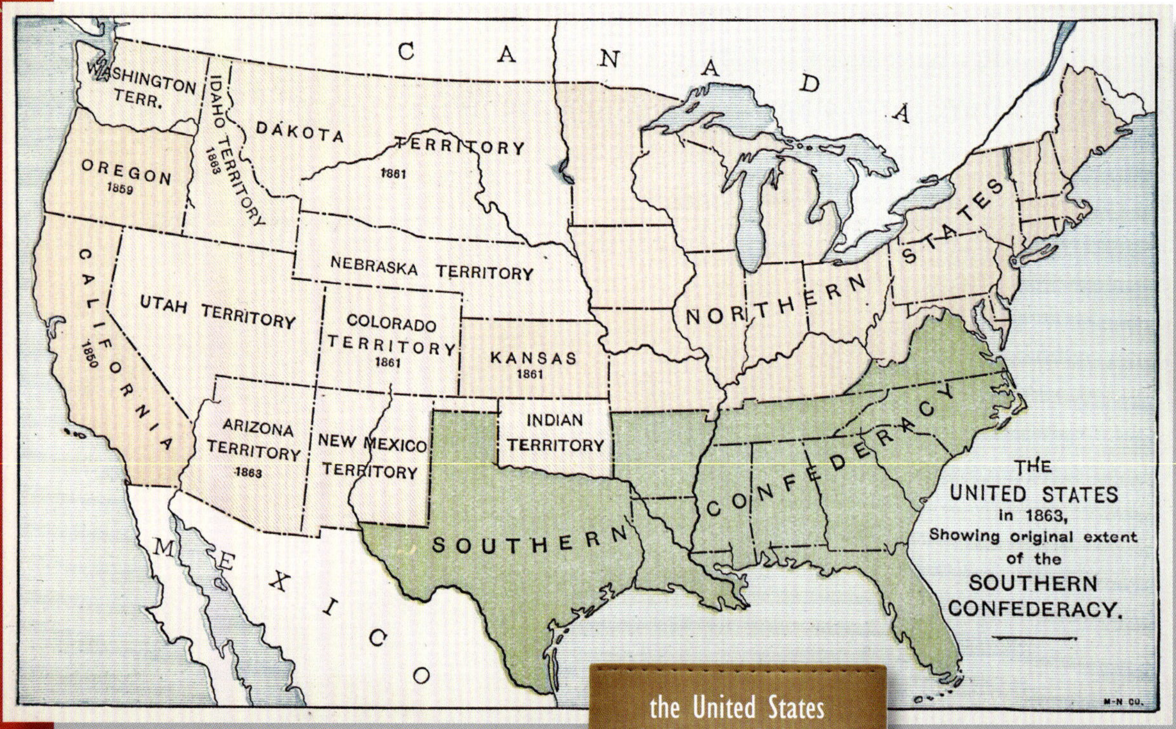

the United States during the Civil War

the amended Texas state constitution

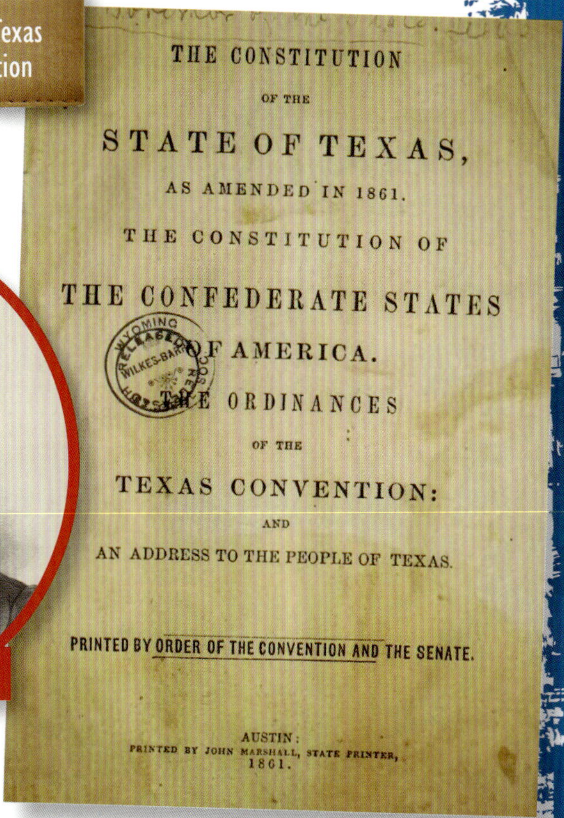
THE CONSTITUTION

OF THE

STATE OF TEXAS,

AS AMENDED IN 1861.

THE CONSTITUTION OF

THE CONFEDERATE STATES

OF AMERICA.

THE ORDINANCES

OF THE

TEXAS CONVENTION:

AND

AN ADDRESS TO THE PEOPLE OF TEXAS.

PRINTED BY ORDER OF THE CONVENTION AND THE SENATE.

AUSTIN:
PRINTED BY JOHN MARSHALL, STATE PRINTER,
1861.

Abraham Lincoln

Sam Houston

Texas seceded from the Union in February 1861. Most Texans by this time did not own slaves. Still, many Texans supported slavery. They felt it was central to the state's economy.

Texas soon joined the Confederate States of America. The Texas Constitution of 1845 was amended, or changed, to create the Constitution of 1861. This new constitution defended slavery and states' rights more strongly. For example, the new constitution made it illegal to free slaves in Texas.

Houston's Warning

Not everyone in Texas supported secession. Sam Houston (HYOO-stuhn), governor of Texas from 1859 to 1861, opposed it. Houston warned Texas that the North would win the Civil War. When Texas seceded, Houston refused to pledge loyalty to the Confederacy. So the Texas Convention forced Houston to step down as governor.

Free Texas

Not all of Texas depended upon slave labor. Large sections of Texas were free of slaves in 1860. In these areas, the economy depended on corn, wheat, and livestock. Farming these crops was not as labor-intensive as farming cotton.

The Civil War Begins

In early 1861, Union troops were stationed at Fort Sumter (SUHM-ter), in Charleston Harbor, South Carolina. When South Carolina seceded, the remaining Union troops were left **vulnerable**, or open to harm. President Lincoln wanted to send supplies to the troops. He told South Carolina about his plans, but the Confederate state did not trust Lincoln. They feared he had plans to attack the South.

On April 11, Confederate forces called for the **surrender** of Fort Sumter. The fort's leader, Major Robert Anderson, refused to give up. He wanted to stay until supplies ran out. On April 12, the Confederates opened fire. After less than two days of fighting, Union forces surrendered the fort.

the attack on Fort Sumter, 1861

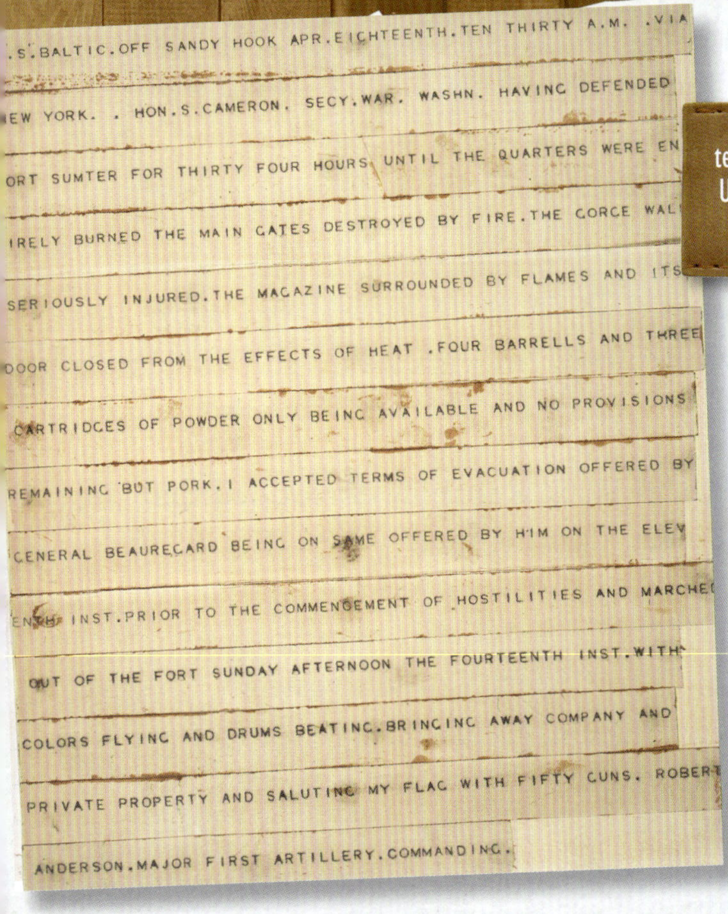
.S. BALTIC. OFF SANDY HOOK APR. EIGHTEENTH. TEN THIRTY A.M. .VIA
EW YORK. . HON. S. CAMERON. SECY. WAR. WASHN. HAVING DEFENDED
ORT SUMTER FOR THIRTY FOUR HOURS UNTIL THE QUARTERS WERE EN
IRELY BURNED THE MAIN GATES DESTROYED BY FIRE. THE CORCE WAL
SERIOUSLY INJURED. THE MAGAZINE SURROUNDED BY FLAMES AND ITS
DOOR CLOSED FROM THE EFFECTS OF HEAT . FOUR BARRELLS AND THREE
CARTRIDCES OF POWDER ONLY BEING AVAILABLE AND NO PROVISIONS
REMAINING BUT PORK. I ACCEPTED TERMS OF EVACUATION OFFERED BY
GENERAL BEAUREGARD BEING ON SAME OFFERED BY HIM ON THE ELEV
ENTH INST. PRIOR TO THE COMMENCEMENT OF HOSTILITIES AND MARCHE
OUT OF THE FORT SUNDAY AFTERNOON THE FOURTEENTH INST. WITH
COLORS FLYING AND DRUMS BEATING. BRINGING AWAY COMPANY AND
PRIVATE PROPERTY AND SALUTING MY FLAG WITH FIFTY GUNS. ROBERT
ANDERSON. MAJOR FIRST ARTILLERY. COMMANDING.

telegram from Major Anderson to the U.S. Secretary of War informing him of the attack on Fort Sumter

The Battle of Fort Sumter ended quickly, and there were no **casualties**. But it was an important battle. Both sides thought they had been pushed into war by the other side. The South felt Lincoln had forced it to attack by sending supplies to Fort Sumter. South Carolina thought it should control the fort since the state had left the Union. The North felt that Confederates started the war by attacking a **federal** fort. But both sides agreed that Fort Sumter marked the start of war.

Texans Join the Fight

About 25,000 Texans joined the Confederate Army in 1861. Many Texas ranchers joined the fight. They left their cattle free to roam the plains so they could fight for the Confederate cause.

Defending the Southwest

Around 90,000 Texans fought for the Confederacy during the Civil War. Most soldiers from Texas stayed in the Southwest. Texans helped the Confederate Army defend against American Indian attacks and kept the Union Army out of the region.

The War Comes to Texas

Texas did not escape the fighting during the Civil War. Galveston (GAL-vuh-stuhn) Harbor was the largest seaport in Texas. Union leaders knew it was an important **port** to control. On October 4, 1862, Union troops entered Galveston. Texas Confederates tried to defend the port, but Union forces were too strong. Union Commander W. B. Renshaw demanded that Confederates surrender the port. His demand was part of a larger plan. The Union wanted to stop goods from coming into and going out of Texas.

For a short time, the Union had control of Galveston, but in November, Major General John Bankhead Magruder (muh-GROO-der) took charge of the Confederate troops. He wanted to take the port back for the Confederacy.

gunboats fighting in the Battle of Galveston

By the President of the United States of America:

A Proclamation.

Whereas, on the twenty-second day of September, in the year of our Lord one thousand eight hundred and sixty-two, a proclamation was issued by the President of the United States, containing, among other things, the following, to wit:

"That on the first day of January, in the year of our Lord one thousand eight hundred "and sixty-three, all persons held as slaves within "any State or designated part of a State, the people "whereof shall then be in rebellion against the "United States, shall be then, thenceforward, and "forever free; and the Executive Government of the "United States, including the military a
"authority thereof, will recognize and
"the freedom of such persons, and will
"or acts to repress such persons, or any of them, "in any efforts they may make for their actual "freedom.

"That the Executive will, on the first day

Emancipation Proclamation

Magruder ordered a naval attack on Union troops at Galveston. He also ordered a sneak attack over a bridge. Former Texas Revolutionary fighter Thomas Green helped in the attack. The Confederates entered the port by ship on January 1, 1863. They opened fire and won control of Galveston Harbor. Unlike Fort Sumter, this battle was deadly. The Confederacy lost 26 men, and 117 more were wounded. The Union lost around 600 men.

Emancipation Proclamation

On January 1, 1863, President Lincoln issued the Emancipation Proclamation. This was the same day Confederates fired on Galveston. The proclamation stated that all slaves in Confederate states were now free. This did not actually free any slaves since the Confederates did not honor the law. However, it let African Americans join the Union Army. And if a slave escaped to the North, he or she could not be returned.

Conscription Law

By April 1862, the Confederates badly needed troops. So the Confederacy passed a **conscription** law. This law forced men to join the military. Many Texans were not in favor of the law. But Texas governor Francis Lubbock (LUHB-uhk) supported it.

Success for the South

Union gunboats attack Fort Griffin in the Battle of Sabine Pass

The early part of the Civil War went well for the Confederacy. The South won important battles in the first years of the war. The Confederate success lasted even longer in Texas.

Later in 1863, the Confederacy had another victory in the Battle of Sabine (SEY-bahyn) Pass. On September 8, Union troops entered the area by ship, planning to travel the Sabine River. They hoped to block a railroad that led out of Houston. But to do this, they first needed to take over Fort Griffin. This was a Confederate fort where Southern men had been sent as punishment.

There were only 44 men at Fort Griffin. They spent their time firing **artillery** (ahr-TIL-uh-ree), or large weapons, into the river. When the Union troops approached, the Confederates were ready. Led by Lieutenant Richard W. Dowling, the Confederates forced the Union troops to stop. They took about 200 Union troops as prisoners.

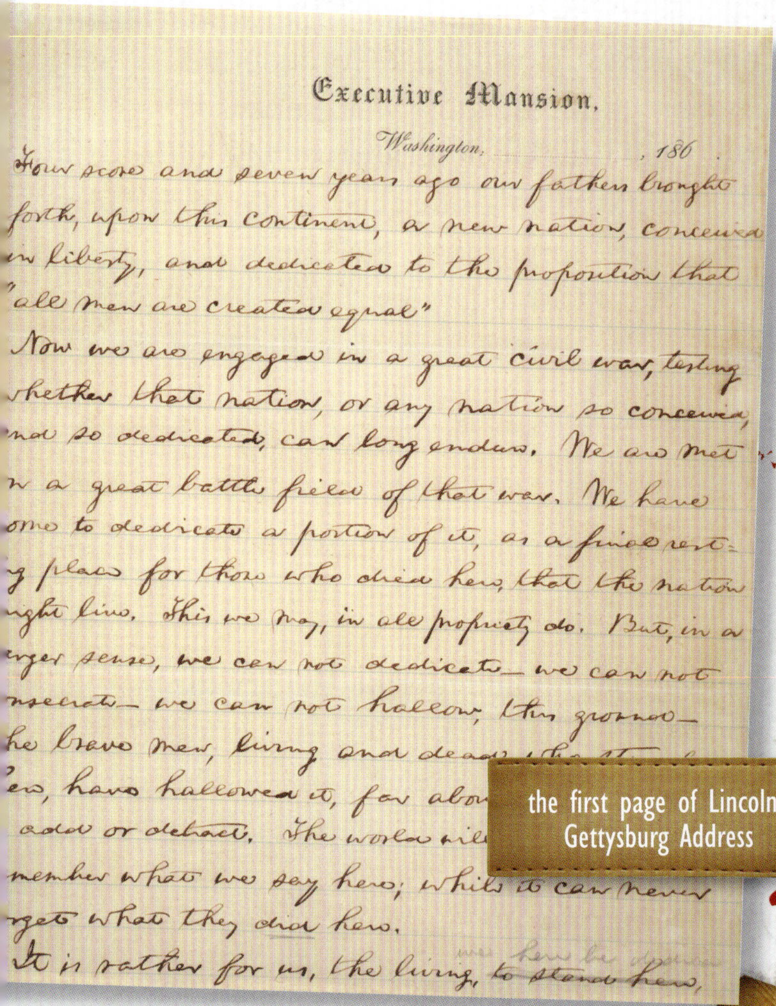

Executive Mansion,

Washington, , 186

Four score and seven years ago our fathers brought
forth, upon this continent, a new nation, conceived
in liberty, and dedicated to the proposition that
"all men are created equal"
Now we are engaged in a great civil war, testing
hether that nation, or any nation so conceived,
nd so dedicated, can long endure. We are met
n a great battle field of that war. We have
ome to dedicate a portion of it, as a final rest-
g place for those who died here, that the nation
ight live. This we may, in all propriety do. But, in a
rger sense, we can not dedicate— we can not
nsecrate— we can not hallow, this ground—
he brave men, living and dead,
ere, have hallowed it, far abov
add or detract. The world wil
member what we say here; while it can never
rget what they did here.
It is rather for us, the living, to stand here,

the first page of Lincoln's Gettysburg Address

John Bell Hood

John Bell Hood

Although he was born in Kentucky, John Bell Hood saw Texas as his home. During the Civil War, Hood became a leader in the Confederate Army. In 1942, the U. S. Army opened a fort in Killeen, Texas, and named it Fort Hood.

Gettysburg Address

On November 19, 1863, President Abraham Lincoln delivered the Gettysburg Address. The speech addressed the question of whether the United States could continue as a united nation based on equality. He called upon the nation to live up to the Founding Fathers' idea of a land of liberty for all people.

The War Ends

Confederates won many battles early in the war. But over time, it became clear that the Union was stronger. The North had too many resources for the South to win. By the summer of 1863, Union forces started to control the war.

The Union was winning, but the Confederates continued to defend Texas. On May 11, 1865, Colonel Theodore H. Barrett and Lieutenant Colonel David Branson led Union troops in an attack on Confederate troops. The battle took place on Brazos (BRAH-zohs) Island in south Texas.

The next day, Union troops surrounded a Confederate **outpost**. But they soon learned the outpost was empty. It was late at night, and Branson led the troops to a place where they could sleep along the Rio Grande. The next morning, **civilians** warned the Confederates that Union troops were there. But Branson found out and led an attack on a Confederate camp at Palmito (PAHLM-ee-toh) Ranch.

Colonel Theodore H. Barrett

The Battle of Palmito Ranch was the last battle of the Civil War. It resulted in a Confederate victory on May 13, 1865. But it was too late. The South had already lost the Civil War.

a group of African American Union soldiers

John Wilkes Booth kills President Lincoln.

African American Troops

More than 180,000 African Americans fought for the Union during the Civil War. In addition to fighting Confederates for freedom, they fought against unequal treatment and unequal pay in the Union Army.

Death of a President

President Lincoln was shot on April 14, 1865, while watching a play at Ford's Theater in Washington, DC. He died the next day. His killer was John Wilkes Booth, a well-known actor and Confederate supporter. Booth and other Confederates secretly planned to kill the president, vice president, and secretary of state. But they were only successful in killing Lincoln.

Rebuilding Texas

After the Civil War, the United States went through many changes. This period of change after the war was called *Reconstruction*. Texas went through these changes, too.

In June 1865, the U.S. Army took over Texas. The goal was to protect **emancipated** (ih-MAN-suh-pey-tid), or freed, African Americans. Freedom meant new kinds of relations between African Americans and white people in Texas. Many white people had a hard time treating former slaves as their equals. The United States wanted to make sure Texas would be loyal to the nation and respect the new laws and ways of living.

buffalo soldiers after the Civil War

In 1866, six regiments of African American troops were added to the U.S. Army. These soldiers served many roles in Texas. They helped rebuild the state and enforce the new rules. American Indians called these troops "buffalo soldiers." It was a respectful name because American Indians respected bison. As soldiers, African Americans earned more money than they could make in most other jobs. They also earned respect from army officers who had doubted them.

buffalo soldier leader Henry O. Flipper

Henry O. Flipper

Trailblazer

Henry O. Flipper was born a slave in Georgia in 1856. In 1877, he became the first African American to graduate from the United States Military Academy at West Point. He also became the first African American officer to lead buffalo soldiers. He led troops in Texas for the rest of his military career.

Economic Changes

The end of slavery also affected the Texas economy. Cotton farmers no longer had free labor. Now, farmers could not make enough money growing cotton. Texans tried to grow other crops and livestock. They grew wheat and corn and raised cattle and sheep.

cowboys on a cattle drive

Cattle and Cowboys

The Rise of the Cattle Industry

The Texas cattle industry began to grow after the Civil War. Texans had led cattle drives before the war, but in 1866, more ranchers began hiring cowboys to drive their cattle to other states where livestock could be sold at higher prices.

Ranchers opened new trails for cattle drives. Jesse Chisholm (CHIZ-uhm), a trader who was part **Cherokee** (CHER-uh-kee), **blazed** an early trail. The trail was expanded to lead from the Rio Grande in Texas north to Kansas. By 1867, it was known as the Chisholm Trail.

In 1866, ranchers Charles Goodnight and Oliver Loving blazed another route from Texas. It led through New Mexico and Colorado to Wyoming. This trail became known as the Goodnight-Loving Trail. In 1874, cattle driver John T. Lytle (LIT-uhl) blazed a trail called the *Western Trail* that led from Texas to Nebraska.

In 1866, cowboys drove nearly 300,000 cattle along trails out of Texas. When the cattle industry was at its height, even larger cattle drives took place. The largest drive was in 1871 when about 700,000 cattle were moved along trails from Texas to Kansas.

Jesse Chisholm

Quanah Parker

Quanah (KWAH-nuh) Parker was the son of a Comanche (kuh-MAN-chee) chief and Cynthia Ann Parker. His mother was a white girl who was kidnapped by Comanches when she was nine years old. During his life, Quanah served as a bridge between the Comanche and the U. S. government and culture.

Indian Outrage

Quanah Parker was a Comanche leader. In 1867, he refused to sign the Medicine Lodge Treaty. The treaty said that Comanches had to live on a reservation as farmers. For the next seven years, Parker led raids against white people in Texas and Mexico. In 1875, Quanah Parker surrendered. His Comanche people moved to a reservation.

King Ranch

Richard King was a riverboat captain. He came to Texas during the Mexican-American War. After the war, King dominated the Rio Grande trade and began to buy Texas land. During the Civil War, he bought a large ranch. This was the start of King Ranch. King Ranch would become the largest ranch in Texas. Today, King Ranch is larger than the state of Rhode Island!

The Chuck Wagon

Charles Goodnight invented the chuck wagon for use on cattle drives. It had special compartments for carrying food and counters that could be used to prepare food. It also carried tools, bedding, water, and utensils.

Cowboy Life

Texas cowboys came from different walks of life. Many Civil War veterans became cowboys. Freed slaves became cowboys. Runaways and drifters became cowboys, too. No matter where they came from, cowboys had to be strong and tough to handle their jobs.

cowboys eating from a chuck wagon

Cattle were not easy to control on drives. They sometimes spread out across two miles (3 km) of land. When this happened, cowboys had to surround the animals at different points. They communicated with their fellow workers by using hand signals borrowed from American Indian sign language. They also gestured with their hats.

a cattle drive in the 1870s

Cowboys worked in crews of about 12 men and managed 2,000 to 3,000 cattle. Drives often covered 10 to 15 miles (16–24 km) each day and took around 25 to 100 days to complete. Cowboys were not the only people who drove cattle. Cowgirls drove cattle, too. Sometimes, they dressed as men to disguise themselves.

One of the most successful Texas cowgirls of the 1870s and 1880s was Lizzie Johnson. She made cattle her business and never disguised herself. Lizzie bought her own herd and had her own brand. She became one of the first women to drive her herd along the Chisholm Trail.

cowgirl Lizzie Johnson

Cowboys try to escape a cattle stampede.

Dangers on the Trail

Texas cowboys faced harsh conditions on cattle drives. They had to handle their herds in all kinds of weather. During dry times, they struggled to find water for the animals and for themselves. During rainy periods, they had trouble crossing flooded rivers. Drowning was a real threat. Lightning and thunder could also cause problems by scaring cattle. Frightened cattle sometimes led to a **stampede** (stam-PEED). The animals would run wild and scatter. Before they were rounded up, they could easily kill cowboys by trampling them.

There were other dangers on the trails, too. In parts of Texas, cowboys might face American Indian attacks. They also had to watch out for rattlesnakes. A rattlesnake bite could be deadly.

rattlesnake

When cowboys were injured or became ill on the trail, they had to rely on homemade cures. A typical cure for a rattlesnake bite in the 1800s was to cut the skin around the bite. Then, the poison could be squeezed or sucked out of the wound. When cowboys got other kinds of wounds, they applied a prickly-pear cactus **poultice** (POHL-tis), or soft pack. To stay healthy on the trail, cowboys often drank bison-meat juice!

a railroad construction crew in 1886

James Hogg

Railroad Hogg

In 1891, James Hogg became the first native, or Texas-born, governor of Texas. He helped establish the Railroad Commission of Texas. Chaired by John H. Reagan, the Railroad Commission prevented Texas railroad monopolies. A **monopoly** is the complete control of a market by one company or person.

Expanding Railroads

Railroad construction after the Civil War extended train service in Texas. Railroad expansion greatly affected the Western territories. New towns sprang up and old towns died off as railroads sprawled around the country. By 1872, the Texas railroad system was connected to railroads serving the rest of the United States.

End of an Era

Cattle drives did not last as a major part of the Texas economy. Problems with the system began as early as the 1850s. Texas cattle were not allowed to enter some states. The cattle sometimes carried a deadly disease that could spread to other cattle. Harsh winters in the late 1880s made travel by trail very dangerous. By the late 1880s, new railroads meant there was less need to drive cattle to distant markets. The meat could be shipped to other states in refrigerated train cars.

When it closed in 1884, more than five million cattle had traveled the Chisholm Trail. About two million cattle had traveled the Western Trail by the time it closed in 1894. Use of the Goodnight-Loving Trail ended in the early 1880s.

cattle drive out of Texas

poster for Buffalo Bill's Wild West show

By 1900, cowboys who roamed the open range were a **relic** of the past. Some joined Wild West Shows. In these shows, they could use their skills performing for audiences. Over time, Wild West Shows evolved into rodeo shows. In this way, the cowboy **legacy** lives on in modern Texas.

rodeo show in Texas

Buffalo Bill's Wild West Show

William F. Cody, also known as Buffalo Bill, organized Buffalo Bill's Wild West show in 1883. His shows featured famous cowboys, cowgirls, and American Indians. They traveled all over the United States. The show traveled throughout Texas until 1915.

Barbed Wire

The widespread use of barbed wire in the 1880s also led to the end of cattle drives. Barbed wire divided up the open range. Barbed wire also closed routes to trails cowboys used. Many farmers and small ranchers moved into the growing Texas cities.

barbed wire

Glossary

annexed—took over a territory and made it part of a larger territory

antebellum—the time period before the Civil War

artillery—large weapons (such as cannons) used by the military

blazed—created a route

boom—large growth in an economic industry in a short period of time

casualties—members of the military lost to death, illness, or injury

Cherokee—an American Indian tribe

civilians—people who are not part of the military

conscription—mandatory enrollment in the military

constitution—a written statement outlining the basic laws for a state or country

emancipated—free from slavery

ethnic—shared traditions and values of a group

federal—relating to the U. S. government

fugitive—someone who has run away illegally

lariat—a long rope with a noose; also called a *lasso*

legacy—something handed down from the past

missionaries—people who share their religious faith with others, usually in other countries

monopoly—complete control of a market by one company or person

outpost—a station at a distance from the main army camp

port—a harbor town or city where ships load or unload cargo

poultice—a soft pack made with herbs, bread, cloth, or other materials that is applied to the body as medicine

profit—money made in business

relic—a part of the past

republic—a separate country

saddle horns—leather grips found near the front of a saddle

secede—to leave a country and form a new government

stamina—a person's ability to do physical work over a long period of time

stampede—a sudden rush made by animals

surrender—to give over the power, control, or possession of another, especially by force

treaty—a legal agreement between two governments

vulnerable—in a position that is open to danger

Index

Your Turn!

After the Civil War, many African American soldiers joined the U. S. Army. These soldiers served many roles in Texas. They helped rebuild the war-torn state. They enforced the new laws. As a sign of respect, the local American Indians began calling them "buffalo soldiers."

We Want You!

Design a poster advertising jobs for African Americans in the U. S. Army. Be sure to list the positives about joining the U. S. Army to attract more soldiers.